Amir & Stacy —

Have a sweet new year!

Here's a quick and easy way
to inspire each day!

All the best,
Zalman Gerber

By Mendel Kalmenson, culled from the *My Encounter with the Rebbe* project

Cover Art by Annita Soble

Cover and book design by Hannabi Creative

Printed in the United States of America by The Printhouse

First Impression, June 2016

ISBN 9781932349023

Dedicated to the Rebbe,
whose seeds of wisdom continue
to be nurtured in the lives of so many.

Joyfully sponsored by
Dr. Michael S. Maling
and the Crain-Maling Foundation

SEEDS OF WISDOM | 2

Culled from *My Encounter with the Rebbe* interviews

JEWISH EDUCATIONAL MEDIA

· SECTION I ·

NURTURING THE HUMAN SPIRIT

· SECTION 2 ·

INSPIRING OTHERS

GROWTH AND DEVELOPMENT

· SECTION 4 ·

CONNECTING TO THE DIVINE

· SECTION 5 ·

LOVE AND RELATIONSHIPS

· SECTION 6 ·

JEWISH LEADERSHIP

· PREFACE ·

A hallmark of the Rebbe's philosophy was his insistence
that the Torah is not merely a book of text, but a textbook
for life. Axiomatic to the Rebbe's worldview was his
deep-seated belief that more than simply a *repository* of
knowledge and wisdom, the Torah is a cosmic *respiratory*
system, breathing life and light into our collective and
personal universe alike.

And no where is this more evident than in the hundreds
of thousands of personal exchanges he had with people
from all walks of life, who sought his counsel on a wide
variety of life's questions and challenges, sensing in him a
wise and compassionate conduit of divine wisdom.

In the warm exchanges that follow, you will encounter
examples of how one spiritual leader took the Torah out
of the Holy Ark and into troubled hearts, transporting its
wisdom from static scrolls to live situations, from ink to
incubator, from the academic to the applicable, providing
the Human context for Heavenly texts.

To be clear, the purpose of this book is not to share the Rebbe's history (his-story) but to inspire positive, meaningful change and growth in yours. Allow me to invite you to take the next step in the epic journey of bringing the Torah down to earth, by unpacking the seeds of wisdom contained in this book, and planting them in the garden of your life.

—MENDEL KALMENSON
London, 2016

· A NOTE ·

I'd like to make an important observation about the stories in this book.

If there's one rule I've learned from researching the Rebbe's responses to people and situations, it is that there are no rules. More than he answered questions, the Rebbe had a knack for answering people. His genius lay not in bundling people and situations together, but in discerning and appreciating the subtleties of each dilemma—seeing how each person and every situation was unique.

These stories are therefore presented as relevant and thought-provoking personal encounters with the Rebbe, not universal advice to be applied in every similar situation. Also, the often whimsical one-line takeaways at the end of each story are no more than my own interpretations. They're intended as points of departure to help you apply the meaning of the story, rather than as final destinations. Not everyone will glean the same lessons from every story. I've tried to stick with "universal truisms," but ultimately each person and every situation is unique.

M.K.

· THE REBBE ·

The Lubavitcher Rebbe, Rabbi Menachem Mendel Schneerson (1902-1994), of righteous memory, was the seventh leader in the Chabad-Lubavitch dynasty.

He is considered one of the most influential religious personalities of modern times. People of all faiths, nationalities and backgrounds sought his advice and counsel, traveling from across the world to receive his blessing and guidance.

More than any other individual, the Rebbe was responsible for stirring the conscience of world Jewry, leading to a spiritual awakening that continues to be felt today.

To his hundreds of thousands of followers and millions of admirers around the world, he was—and remains today, following his passing—"the Rebbe."

NURTURING THE HUMAN SPIRIT

TRUE HAPPINESS

The thirteen-year-old daughter of a Jewish leader wrote a letter to the Rebbe in anticipation of a scheduled meeting between her father and the Rebbe.

"Dear Rebbe, like many other righteous people, my father has a great wish to live in the Land of Israel... Please make my father happy by giving him your consent and blessing to make *aliyah*."

In his long and sensitive response, the Rebbe acknowledged the girl's feelings, but gently explained the importance of her father's work in his community: "...I am gratified to note your profound concern for your parents. Knowing your father, I have no doubt that he will feel in his element only in a place where he can fully utilize his knowledge and qualities for the benefit of the many. Based on this, you will surely realize that he will be *truly* happy if he continues in his present situation and country."

True happiness comes from fulfilling your potential, not your desires.

SPEAKING ILL OF ONESELF

A man visiting the Rebbe bemoaned his spiritual state. "Rebbe, something must be wrong with me! I have spent a lot of time in the company of saintly individuals, but their example doesn't seem to affect me. I must be insensitive to spirituality!"

The Rebbe interjected, "Just as it is forbidden to speak disparagingly about someone else—even if one speaks the absolute truth—it is also forbidden to speak negatively about oneself!"

 If it doesn't propel you forward, don't dwell on it.

THE MOST INTIMATE CONFIDANT

Rabbi Tzvi Hirsh Weinreb moved with his family to Maryland to pursue a career in psychology. At one point he was going through a difficult time, and decided to call the Rebbe for guidance.

The Rebbe's secretary answered the phone, and asked the caller to identify himself.

Not wanting to disclose his name due to the sensitive nature of his questions, Rabbi Weinreb replied only, "A Jew from Maryland." He went on to outline the questions for which he wanted the Rebbe's guidance—uncertainties regarding his life, his career and faith.

Suddenly, Rabbi Weinreb heard the Rebbe's voice in the background: "Tell him there's a Jew in Maryland with whom he can speak. His name is Weinreb."

The secretary repeated the Rebbe's words. "Yes," he exclaimed to the secretary, "but... *my* name is Weinreb!"

Rabbi Weinreb then heard the Rebbe saying gently: "If that's the case, he should know that sometimes one needs to speak to himself."

 Deep down, you already know the answer.

FEEDBACK

On major Jewish holidays, the Rebbe called on his *chasidim* to go on foot to the hundreds of synagogues within walking distance of Lubavitch Headquarters, and bring joy and inspiration to other communities. As a gesture of gratitude, the Rebbe gave out "wine of blessing" to all of those who had participated.

Once, a *chasid* who was the rabbi of a synagogue in another neighborhood joined the line to receive this special wine. When his turn came, he explained to the Rebbe, "I, too, shared words of inspiration in my synagogue." With a smile, the Rebbe replied, "Yes, but you receive a salary for speaking to your congregation."

"Perhaps," said the rabbi, "but the speech that I gave was worth far more than what I'm being paid for it!"

"That," said the Rebbe good-naturedly, "is for them to judge, not you."

You cannot be objective about something as subjective as yourself.

ANGEL'S ENVY

A rabbinical student from Sydney Australia once visited the Rebbe to discuss his spiritual growth. During their discussion, the Rebbe said, "You should know that the heavenly angels, despite their great spiritual elevation, envy you when you walk down bustling Bondi Junction wearing your *kipah* and *tzizit* proudly for all to see!"

 You earn the respect of others when you respect yourself.

THE FASTER WAY

One Wednesday evening, a woman told the Rebbe that she had taken a vow to fast on Mondays and Thursdays as a form of penitence for her past. The Rebbe grew serious and said, "Fasting as a method of spiritual development is not the *chasidic* way. Please have your vow annulled tonight, so that you can eat already tomorrow morning."

Sensing the woman's reluctance to give up this spiritual practice, the Rebbe said, "If you are looking for a form of repentance—instead of not eating at all, I would suggest that you forego one food item that you crave for six days of the week, and enjoy it on Shabbat."

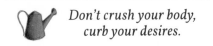

Don't crush your body,
curb your desires.

WORK IN PROGRESS

A man whose children attended *yeshivah*, once observed some students behaving inappropriately. When he met with the Rebbe, he remarked: "Such behavior might be understandable in secular university students. But if *yeshivah* students behave this way, it seems to point to a deficiency in their education."

The Rebbe replied, "If one observes an individual walking into a doctor's office in perfect health and then leaving the treatment unable to walk, one might assume that the doctor and the medicine may be flawed. But if one observes a patient in the midst of treatment, one cannot yet draw any conclusions as to the effectiveness of the medication.

"The students you observed are in the midst of their education, and each day they are learning to be a little bit better."

 Judaism demands progression, not perfection.

PRESENCE

A couple who had moved from Crown Heights to London as emissaries of the Rebbe experienced a setback and were feeling discouraged. They decided to move back to Crown Heights, at least temporarily, to regain their confidence and drive. Before finalizing their plans, the woman wrote to the Rebbe saying that she and her husband wanted to move back in order to be "in the Rebbe's environment and presence."

In his response, the Rebbe circled the words "in the Rebbe's environment and presence" and wrote, "Certainly it is the spiritual that you have in mind, not the wood and stone of the neighborhood. This you will find in my institutions in London."

 "You are where your thoughts are."
—THE BAAL SHEM TOV[1]

DO SOMETHING

The Rebbe once encouraged a visitor to add in his Shabbat observance. "But Rebbe, I have never kept Shabbat before," the man countered, "it would be too difficult a change!"

The Rebbe responded: "Even if you feel that complete Shabbat observance is currently beyond your ability, why don't you start by taking upon yourself to honor Shabbat by abstaining from just one prohibited act that you otherwise would have done?"

 You might not be able to do everything, but you can always do something.

CHANGE YOUR MIND

A woman who had converted to Judaism once came to see the Rebbe to discuss a personal matter. "Rebbe, sometimes I am visited by thoughts or hymns from my former religion and this disturbs me greatly, especially when I am engaged in prayer. What can I do to prevent these unwanted thoughts from entering my mind?"

"The mind cannot think two different thoughts at the same time," the Rebbe responded. "The next time you want to get rid of a thought, don't try to fight it; simply replace it with a different one."

 You can't control who comes knocking on your door, but you can control who you let in.

MITZVOT EVERYWHERE

At the end of a meeting, the Rebbe handed a dollar bill to a young woman from overseas. "This is to be given to charity," referring to the custom of making someone the agent of a *mitzvah* before they travel, so that the merit of the *mitzvah* will protect them on their journey. The young woman, who was studying in Crown Heights at the time, responded, "But I'm not traveling anywhere!"

With a smile the Rebbe replied, "Then give it as *shliach mitzvah gelt* in Crown Heights, because Crown Heights is also in need of *mitzvot.*"

 Charity begins at home.

COMMEMORATE OR CELEBRATE?

Dr. Robert Feldman was a physician who treated the Rebbe's wife, Rebbetzin Chaya Mushka. In the winter of 1988, Dr. Feldman's daughter Sarah became engaged. The Rebbetzin, who had advised Sarah while she was dating, was delighted with the good news.

A short while later, the Rebbetzin passed away, and the Rebbe grieved over her passing. During the *shiva*, the Rebbe sent for Dr. Feldman. "Tell me, when is the engagement party?" he asked.

This wasn't a simple question. The party was originally scheduled to take place within the thirty days of mourning of the Rebbetzin's passing. However, to delay the happy occasion was no small matter either. Before Dr. Feldman could answer, the Rebbe continued: "It should take place on the day it was originally scheduled, and it should not be smaller than originally planned. In fact, it should be bigger! The main thing is, it should celebrated with great joy."

The Rebbe's tone then softened, and with emotion he said, "This is how the Rebbetzin would have wanted it to be, and this is what will make her happy."

We honor those who have passed not by maintaining the void created by their loss, but by filling it with life.

OF BLESSED MEMORY

A couple who had recently lost their young daughter came to see the Rebbe in search of answers.

"Rebbe," the grieving father asked, "how can we find solace?"

"You will find comfort through the initiatives and activities you implement in your daughter's merit."

"But remember," cautioned the Rebbe, "don't confuse honoring her memory with the things you do to bring merit to her soul."

The Rebbe explained, "Sometimes people are more concerned that the name of a loved one be engraved on the *outside* of a building, than they are with the positive activities being done *inside* the building, which bring spiritual satisfaction and elevation to the soul."

A departed soul is nourished
not through fame,
but through the good deeds
we do in his or her name.

SELECTIVE MEMORY

Visiting Camp Gan Israel, the boy's summer camp he had founded, the Rebbe surveyed the grounds. Stopping in front of a small bunk house used to store old and broken items, the Rebbe peeked inside. The words carved onto the wall by a witty staff member caught his attention: *"zecher l'churban,"* it said. "In remembrance of the destruction of the Holy Temple."

The Rebbe turned to his tour guide and suggested a positive spin: "Why mention the destruction? You can just write *'zecher l'mikdash'* – In remembrance of the Holy Temple."

 Don't dwell on what you've lost, remember what you've been given.

LESSONS IN CHESS

Once, during a *chasidic* gathering of the Rebbe attended by the world-famous chess grandmaster, Sam Rashevsky, the Rebbe observed: "*Chasidic* philosophy encourages us to derive a lesson from everything we see and hear in the world around us. What spiritual lesson can be learned in the service of G-d from the game of chess?

"...There are two types of players in the game. There are 'officers'—the queen, knight, bishop and rook—and there are 'soldiers,' or pawns. The difference between them is that officers can jump beyond their particular location and can move in all directions, covering ground quicker than the soldiers who can only move forward in one direction and one square at a time.

"Nevertheless, the foot soldier has a certain characteristic which makes him superior. When a pawn reaches the far side of the board, he can become elevated to the rank of a queen."

"The same is true in the game of life. There are two categories of "players": angels and human beings. The angels have greater powers, and can jump from one spiritual realm to the next. However, they can never transform themselves into something else. Human beings, while limited to taking one step at a time, can eventually transform themselves and reach beyond their natural limitations."

*The winners in life
are not those born kings,
but are those who grow wings.*

LASTING RESOLUTIONS

During a private audience with a young man who was dedicated to self-improvement, the Rebbe observed: "There are two reasons that good resolutions rarely last. The first is that in the hope of dramatic transformation, people take upon themselves changes in behavior that are unrealistic and too difficult. Less is often more; if you want results, it's better to focus on the achievable rather than on the desirable.

"Secondly," the Rebbe continued, "People underestimate the importance of channeling inspiration into *immediate* action. Never push off a good resolution until 'later' or 'tomorrow.' By then the inspiration may have passed, and with it, the power of your resolve."

In Torah, "The word v'ata, 'and now,' always indicates a call to personal change."
—MIDRASH[2]

WHERE'S THE PROBLEM?

A *yeshivah* student from New York was struggling in his studies, and he visited the Rebbe to discuss his challenges. "I'm thinking of enrolling in a *yeshivah* in Israel," the young man suggested. "I'll be less distracted there."

The Rebbe responded with a smile, "When you go somewhere new, your negative inclination travels with you."

 If the problem is inside you, running away won't help.

THE CAUSE OF ALL HEALING

During the Simchat Torah celebrations of 1977, the Rebbe suffered a heart attack. Right after the prayers, he was seen by a number of prominent doctors at his office in 770. The consensus was that the Rebbe must be treated in a hospital. The Rebbe refused, insisting that his treatment and recuperation could be at 770.

"My healing will come from this room," he explained.

"Have you any idea what has transpired here?" asked the Rebbe with emotion. "Do you see this desk and this chair and these books? They have been privy to the tears and hopes of so many...

"These walls have absorbed the energy of people who came for blessings, and they are sacred. This energy will be part of my healing."

*Your well-being
is linked to the fulfillment
of your life's mission.*

SPIRITUAL COMMISSION

A certain individual once helped the Rebbe facilitate the placement of a particular rabbi. Some time later, when the Rebbe saw this person he told him graciously, "I owe you commission for your assistance!"

A number of years later, the man came back. "Rebbe," he said, "You once told me that I'm owed commission. I'd like to request it now in the form of your blessing for financial success."

The Rebbe responded, "You've already been receiving the commission you were promised, in the tremendous *nachas* you are seeing from your children."

 The greatest blessing one can receive is for the things that money can't buy.

A LIVING EDUCATION

The Rebbe once visited a communal Passover *seder* being held at an educational institution in Crown Heights. He turned to the youngest child present and asked, "Do you know the Four Questions by heart?" The boy nodded his head in the affirmative. With a smile, the Rebbe turned to the boy's father and asked, "But do you know the answers?"

The next day, the Rebbe explained to the father: "When I questioned your son, I used the expression 'by heart' intentionally, rather than the Hebrew *"baal peh*—by rote," because children don't connect with ceremonies that are merely memorized."

"On Passover the child asks: 'We did this whole ritual last year, why are we doing it again?' And he's asking it with all his *heart*! That's why I asked your son if he knows the Four Questions *by heart*.

"And my question to *you* was whether you know the answers to *his* questions? Do you know how to answer your child in such a way that he experiences Passover in a new way this year?"

For Judaism to thrive,
not just survive,
it must be celebrated,
not just commemorated.

PRISMS OF REALITY

During a private audience with the Rebbe, a bureau chief for a national Jewish newspaper extolled his periodical. "There is nothing we would not report, even if it meant portraying the Jewish community negatively!" he exclaimed. "Journalism is journalism. When it comes to honest reporting you don't protect your brother or sister.

"Our publication is independent," he concluded, "and completely objective!"

The Rebbe responded pointedly: "Independent, perhaps—but completely objective? There is no such thing. It is humanly impossible to be completely objective. Every person has a bias of some kind."

It is only natural to view the world through a prism. The question is, which prism have you chosen?

· SECTION 2 ·

INSPIRING
OTHERS

A WARM HOME

A newly engaged couple wrote to the Rebbe asking that they be blessed with "a warm home."

Some time later, during a private audience, the Rebbe addressed their letter saying, "See to it that others are warm, and your lives will be warm, as well."

The way to lead an inspired life
is to inspire others.

FULL CYCLE

A young rabbi came to see the Rebbe. "During the course of your career," the Rebbe told him, "it is inevitable that you will officiate at weddings, funerals and mourner's services at *shiva* homes. At these times, when people are most receptive and open, don't focus only on the required rituals and customs, rather, utilize these events to share the beauty of Judaism, and encourage them to live more inspired lives."

*Life-cycle events shouldn't just mark
the outer contours of our journey,
they should fill the contours with light.*

ON THE OFFENSIVE

In the early 1970s a young rabbi visited the Rebbe, seeking his advice. "I recently received an offer to become the rabbi of a congregation in Tennessee, but I have reservations about moving my family to a place with no Jewish environment. My children may stray from Judaism, G-d forbid!"

"To the contrary!" the Rebbe responded, "By being part of the creation of a Jewish environment where there is none, they will become stronger Jews. In fact, they will be stronger than if they were to live within an established religious environment which could be taken for granted."

There's a world of difference between a passive participant and a proactive proponent.

THE BEST KIND OF TEACHER

A rabbinical student met with the Rebbe in a private audience. After a rigorous Talmudic discussion with the bright young man, the Rebbe said, "I can see you have studied well, but I also want you to remember the words of our sages: 'Receive every person with a cheerful countenance.'[3] More than anything else, it will be your warmth and care that will impact the people you meet."

People don't care how much you know,
until they know how much you care.

SPHERE OF INFLUENCE

A congregational rabbi who was at a crossroads in his career visited the Rebbe for guidance. He had been offered a teaching job and was passionate about Jewish education, but he had reservations about leaving the rabbinate. "Should I stay on as a rabbi or should I become a teacher?" he asked. The Rebbe responded, "The question you need to ask yourself is this: 'Where will I be able to have the greatest impact on the largest group of people?'

"In the classroom you will have twenty or thirty students per year, whereas through your work with the community, your sphere of influence extends to many more. If *Hashem* has given you the ability to lead a community, this is the correct choice for you."

Where can you be of most benefit to the largest group of people?

ON BEHALF OF ALL

A rabbi involved in outreach once came to see the
Rebbe for guidance. "I work mainly with young people," he
explained, and elaborated his views on the importance of
engaging youth and building a greater Jewish future.

The Rebbe gently reminded him: "While it is vital
to work with youth, remember not to neglect the older
generation. When Moses petitioned Pharaoh for the
freedom of his people, he did so on behalf of all, declaring:
'With our youth and with our elderly shall we go!'"[4]

*Judaism is not just
concerned with continuity,
but with every individual
within its community.*

BEYOND HUMILITY

A *shliach* was visiting New York and came to see the Rebbe. "Why haven't I heard about your activities?" the Rebbe asked.

"But I just sent you a report detailing my activities!" the surprised *shliach* answered.

"I received it," said the Rebbe, smiling. "But why haven't I read about them in the newspaper? Publicizing a *mitzvah* is a *mitzvah* in itself!"

Publicizing the good that you do allows others to learn from you.

THE BENEFIT OF HELPING OTHERS

A gifted *yeshivah* student came to the Rebbe with a dilemma. Should he stay in *yeshivah* during vacation, as some of his teachers had advised, or should he volunteer at a summer camp for children who weren't given a Jewish education, as many of his friends planned to do?

"It does upset me," he admitted to the Rebbe, "to think of all the time I would be spending teaching kids the basics of Judaism, when I could be furthering my own Torah study instead."

The Rebbe advised him to take the job as counselor. "Our sages teach us that when we devote ourselves to the well-being of others, our heart and mind become a thousand times more refined.[5]

"This isn't poetry," the Rebbe continued, "it is meant literally! If you devote your summer to these children, the same concept in Torah which previously took you a thousand hours to internalize, can take you only one hour."

When you put others before yourself,
G-d places Himself before you.

NUCLEAR REACTION

A young rabbi was involved with outreach projects as well as a fledging business, and was feeling overwhelmed. He visited the Rebbe to discuss which of the areas he should focus on.

To his surprise, the Rebbe replied, "Not only should you not cut back on your activities, you should increase your outreach efforts, your rabbinic work, and also your business."

"I'm humbled and honored by your faith in me," exclaimed the rabbi, "but I don't feel it's realistic for me to manage all these tasks at once!"

The Rebbe looked at him warmly and said, "I'll tell you what your difficulty is. You think that human interactions are like chemical interactions. When two elements interact, they result in the creation of a third compound. But people aren't chemicals. When people interact it's like a nuclear reaction.

"A nuclear reaction has a center, from which further reactions spread in all directions. As the outer rings of that sphere gets larger, the number of reactions grows exponentially. Likewise, when you touch the heart of one person very deeply—even if only for a moment—he in turn will touch many other people, triggering a nuclear explosion of positive influence."

It's not how many people you touch, but how deeply you touch them, that determines your sphere of influence.

THE JEWISH DEFINITION OF LIFE

During a *farbrengen* attended by college professors and university students, the Rebbe remarked, "The Hebrew word for 'life' is *chaim*, which literally means 'lives', in the plural, rather than 'life' in the singular.

"This comes to teach us an important truth. We are not truly alive until we think and care about others."

"If I am for myself, what am I?"
—HILLEL[6]

A TEACHER'S MANUAL

A young man who was about to begin a career in education visited the Rebbe for a blessing. "I understand that you have chosen to become an educator," the Rebbe said to him.

"Correct," the man replied.

"Allow me to share with you what it means to be an educator," offered the Rebbe. "It is not merely to teach information, but to provide your students with faith and a moral compass for life.

"And how does one transmit this to one's students?" the Rebbe mused. "It must come from you. You must take your own 'fear of Heaven' and share it with your students. If you will be a model of passion and purity at all times, that's what they will observe and absorb."

The Rebbe concluded: "Remember, like a well which needs constant replenishing so it doesn't run dry, you need to constantly work on yourself and refill your own reservoir of faith."

Your children will become what you are,
so be what you want them to be.

JUST DO IT

A prolific lecturer on Chasidism once visited the Rebbe to discuss a personal struggle.

"Rebbe," he said, "I don't know if I have enough *Ahavat Yisrael* to be doing what I do. Teaching sometimes makes me feel superior to my audiences, and I feel like my ego has become inflated as a result of my lectures. Perhaps others are better suited for this work."

"Do not hesitate because of these feelings," the Rebbe responded. "When it comes to doing good, action is what's most important."

"Though your donation may lack sincerity, I can assure you, the poor man eats with sincerity."
—THE ALTER REBBE TO A DISCIPLE[7]

THE SECRET BEHIND INFLUENCE

Professor Branover, an acclaimed Russian-Israeli physicist, was once scheduled to address a conference of Jewish scientists. Before leaving for the conference he met with the Rebbe, who told him: "You have an important message to convey. Explain to them that as a scholar of solar energy, you encourage every Jew to emulate the sun.

"Why is this star of such great importance?" the Rebbe continued. "There are larger heavenly bodies, indeed many, which dwarf the sun in size. Other heavenly bodies are also powerful sources of energy. Black holes are extremely powerful, but their energy is directed inward, pulling everything into themselves.

"The sun is unique in that it doesn't just radiate light in isolation; its energy provides warmth to the entire planetary system.

"As the sun gives of itself, so too a Jew must radiate goodness and love upon all human beings."

It doesn't matter if the world considers you large or powerful; is your light and energy radiating upon others?

CLOSE TO G-D

Visitors from an outreach organization once asked
the Rebbe to bless them with success in *"kiruv rechokim—
bringing close those who are far from Judaism."*

The Rebbe's face grew serious.

"I strongly object to the expression. What do we know
about who is close or far? Only G-d can judge these matters.
Besides, nobody is *truly* far from G-d.

"Instead you could call it *kiruv krovim*," said the Rebbe,
his smile returning—"bringing those who are close even
closer."

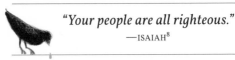

"Your people are all righteous."
—ISAIAH[8]

RULES OF ENGAGEMENT

A Jewish executive who ran a South African ad agency accepted the African National Congress as a client, to help them project a better public image.

One day, while visiting the ANC headquarters, he walked out of an elevator and saw a large poster of Yasser Arafat on the wall. Shocked and dismayed to learn of the ANC's affiliation with terrorists, his friends advised him to ask the Rebbe for guidance.

"Although I have strong liberal and anti-apartheid leanings, I feel like I'm working for the wrong people," he wrote. "Should I continue to work for them or not?"

"Don't stop," the Rebbe replied. "To the contrary, continue working with them, but make every effort to influence them for the good."

The way to fight evil is through illumination, not elimination.

RENEWABLE ENERGY

A community rabbi and his wife were struggling with an immense workload. They wrote to the Rebbe asking if they shouldn't cut back in some areas.

The Rebbe wrote back, "I see in your work a special *zechut* for you and your wife, which also means a channel for G-d's blessing in your needs, materially and spiritually. Therefore, I believe that both of you should try your utmost to continue in your position and work.

"When you increase your activities, you'll widen the channels through which you receive Divine blessings."

The way to generate more light,
is not by conserving oil,
but by squeezing more olives.

TAKE-AWAY

A seasoned rabbi and motivational speaker once shared his self-doubts with the Rebbe. "Rebbe," he said, "I am considered a gifted public speaker and I must have given thousands of talks, yet I wonder: how many of my talks actually hit home? I don't see practical changes in the lives of my listeners."

The Rebbe responded: "Our sages teach, 'Words that come from the heart enter the heart.'[9] If you speak sincerely and with passion, you can be assured that your words will enter people's hearts, whether you see it or not.

"If however, you want to be able to *observe* the actual change you inspire in your audiences," the Rebbe continued, "I suggest that you not speak in abstract terms. Teach your audiences a practical Jewish tradition, and leave them with an action point, even if it's only one thing, and even if it seems minimal. This is how you inspire change."

People might be taken by ideas,
but are given to action.

URGENCY

While discussing campus life with a college student, the Rebbe asked what the Jewish students at the University do about Kosher food.

The man told the Rebbe that the local Hillel House was under construction and its Kosher facilities would not be completed until October.

The Rebbe responded earnestly, "It is now January. And until October is it permissible to eat non-Kosher food?"

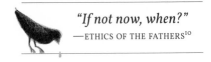

"If not now, when?"
—ETHICS OF THE FATHERS[10]

EMPTY WORDS

The Rebbe once encouraged a man to use his talents to the fullest. At a subsequent meeting, the Rebbe said, "I hope you are fulfilling what we discussed. Don't turn me into a sinner!"

Taken aback, the man asked, "How could I do that?"

"Our sages teach," the Rebbe responded, "'that whoever engages in excessive talk brings on sin.'[11] If our conversation led to no practical outcome, it was merely 'excessive talk.'"

Words are free.
It's how you use them that creates value.

· SECTION 3 ·

GROWTH AND DEVELOPMENT

COMMENCEMENT ADDRESS

A group of high schools girls visited the Rebbe on the occasion of their graduation. The Rebbe told them, "In Jewish tradition, there is a special ceremony for completing the study of a tractate of Mishnah or Talmud called a *siyum*, or 'conclusion.' Immediately after reciting the final passage of the completed text, we commence the study of a new one.

"This comes to teach us an important lesson: the process of learning and acquiring knowledge is never complete; and must continue throughout life."

> *Education is the kindling of a flame, not the filling of a vessel.*

DOLLARS AND SENSE

During a visit to Gan Israel, the boys summer camp he had founded, the Rebbe noticed a large sign on a wall that was meant to humorously encourage visiting parents to tip the waiters. The sign read, "Money is the root of all evil; leave your evil with us!"

The Rebbe asked that the sign be taken down, explaining, "This is not a Jewish quote. In Judaism, money is not seen as the root of evil; if utilized correctly, it can be the root of tremendous good as well."

> *Money is a terrible master but an excellent servant.*

STEP BY STEP

"There's so much talk about *tikkun olam*, repairing the world," said a university student to the Rebbe, "where should I invest my energy—in improving myself or the world?"

"Start with yourself," the Rebbe replied simply. "Then work on your family, your community, then your city and then the world. You be the righteous man, the person of great character, and there will be a ripple effect on the world."

"That's a huge undertaking!" exclaimed the student.

"Let that not stop you," the Rebbe responded. "Be the best person you can be, and take it day by day, one step at a time.

"It's as if there's a basket of fruit suspended from a high ceiling, far beyond your reach. However, you have a ladder. Instead of focusing on the magnitude of the task, climb the ladder step by step, eventually you will reach your goal."

Sometimes, in order to succeed, you need to ignore the big picture.

WIDELY AND WISELY READ

The Rebbe received a visit from an Israeli columnist for the *Algemeiner Journal*, who was known for his sometimes hostile views on religion. Upon meeting him, the Rebbe exclaimed, "I read your column every week!"

Taken aback, the man asked, "Am I to understand that the Rebbe agrees with my views?"

"If I would read only what I agree with," the Rebbe responded with a smile, "I would read precious little."

"Who is wise?
He who learns from everyone."
—ETHICS OF THE FATHERS[12]

EXPANDING YOUR ABILITIES

A director of Jewish education who had recently celebrated his 42nd birthday came to the Rebbe for blessing and counsel. "Rebbe, the pressures of work are getting to me," he said, "and I'm thinking of cutting back on my responsibilities at school. I feel I have taken on too much."

"Too much responsibility?" the Rebbe exclaimed warmly. "There is always room for more! I just celebrated my 70th birthday. Instead of slowing down, I decided to undertake 71 new projects in the coming year. In honor of your recent birthday, how about taking upon yourself 43 new projects?"

We are more capable than we think we are.

REFRAMING

A father encouraged his teenage daughter to join the inaugural class of an advanced Lubavitch girls high school opening in the neighborhood. The girl—feisty by nature—refused to participate, insisting on attending the more established school.

After her father urged her to ask the Rebbe for his advice, she composed a letter describing her reservations. "I do not want to be a guinea pig to be experimented on," she wrote.

The Rebbe's response completely changed the girl's perspective. He simply crossed out the words "guinea pig" and wrote in its place, "pioneer."

A sense of mission
can turn defiance into desire.

RETIREMENT PLANS

The Rebbe asked about the welfare of a visitor's elderly relative, and advised, "See to it that he continues to work, and encourage him to not stop being active."

"But he is already over seventy-years-old!" the man exclaimed, before catching himself—after all, the person across the desk met the same criteria.

With a smile, the Rebbe picked up the thought: "I, too, am more than seventy-years-old, and I have plans for another ten years, and thereafter for another ten!"

> *Old age doesn't bring on inactivity, but inactivity can bring on old age.*

CONSTRUCTIVE SATISFACTION

A *shlucha* who was overwhelmed with her many duties wrote to the Rebbe, describing her feelings of inadequacy. She concluded with the words, "I feel like I'm one big mess."

In response, the Rebbe sent back her letter with the following comment at the bottom: "It's obvious that you and your husband have succeeded in your holy work beyond any conceivable expectation, and you call this"—here the Rebbe drew an arrow pointing to the words he had circled: 'one big mess?!'"

Sometimes, in order to accomplish more, you need to appreciate what you've already achieved.

INSTANT RATIFICATION

A community activist from Berlin visited the Rebbe for Simchat Torah. As the Rebbe was dancing with the Torah scroll, the Rebbe turned to him said, "See to it that Berlin becomes a place filled with *chasidic* warmth!"

"Amen!" he replied, enthusiastically.

The Rebbe continued circling the *bimah*. To the man's astonishment, as the Rebbe passed him again, he smiled and demanded, "Nu, what have you done to implement our recent discussion?"

The next morning, on his way to services, the Rebbe again spotted the individual and said, "At this point, an entire night has gone by! So tell me, what have you accomplished so far?"

---

*Change happens
the moment you decide
that change is going to happen.*

FAST FORWARD

A young rabbinical student who was focused on spiritual growth once asked the Rebbe about the appropriateness of fasting as a means of achieving personal refinement.

"If you want to elevate yourself spiritually," the Rebbe responded, "I would suggest that you abstain from speaking unnecessary words, rather than from eating food."

Are you as careful about what comes out of your mouth as you are with what goes into it?

THE INFINITY OF TORAH

Professor Susan Handelman wrote an article contrasting Torah and secular wisdom. Before it was published, the Rebbe offered to review it and comment. She was honored.

The professor wrote that with perseverance a person can completely master a field of secular knowledge, whereas the Torah, due to its infinite nature, "can never be mastered." On these words, the Rebbe commented in the margin: "Even one *davar*, even one sentence of the Torah (cannot be mastered)."

"Delve and delve into the Torah,
for everything is in it!"
—ETHICS OF THE FATHERS[13]

TORAH NEWS

A journalist for the Israeli radio station Kol Israel, arranged to see the Rebbe. During their discussion the Rebbe suggested that in addition to providing news, Kol Israel should share a weekly insight from the Torah portion with its listeners.

Not convinced, the journalist replied, "Kol Israel is in the business of providing news. Torah is not news!"

The Rebbe responded, "Our sages teach us that every day we must approach Torah as if it were given today.[14] In other words, it's up to us to find the relevance, the connection, between the Torah and our personal lives and current affairs. Therefore if you present each week's Torah portion as it relates to the news, it would indeed be appropriate."

*The Torah doesn't change
from year to year. We do.*

POSITIVE ASSOCIATIONS

Mr. Bentzion Rader was instrumental in publishing a book entitled *Challenge*, which celebrated the activities of Chabad around the world. Upon the project's completion, the Rebbe urged Mr. Rader to publish another book specifically on the efforts of Chabad in Israel.

In a meeting with the Rebbe, Mr. Rader suggested that the new book open with Biblical verses on the unique spiritual qualities of Israel. Sensitive to the fact that the book's intended audience included Jews with minimal connection to the Bible and the Holy Land, the Rebbe responded, "It's a good idea, but be sure to quote only verses which describe the holiness of the Land in positive terms, rather than those describing the consequences of violating its sanctity."

Don't underestimate the power of an association. Like a key, it can open or close the door leading to a new journey.

DON'T DEBATE

Jewish youth in a certain community were being targeted aggressively by missionaries and a concerned community activist asked the Rebbe, "How should we approach Jews who have become involved with Christianity?"

The Rebbe responded, "Don't argue with them about Christianity. Give them something new to think about. Teach them about the beauty and joy of Judaism."

Don't delegitimize.
Open their eyes.

THE DIVINE ORDER

A rabbi whose organization was going through difficult financial times shared his predicament with one of his supporters and asked for a contribution. The individual said that he was involved in a business deal and, if G-d would bless him with success, he would commit to the requested amount.

The rabbi sent a note to the Rebbe asking him to pray on behalf of the potential donor that his business deal might succeed so that he could give the charity.

The Rebbe responded: "Is this the proper way to receive G-d's blessings—by making preconditions with Him? Let him give for the sake of giving, and G-d will do His part."

"Do not be as servants who serve their master for the sake of reward. Rather, be as servants who serve their master not for the sake of reward."—ETHICS OF THE FATHERS[15]

YOUR INNER ANARCHIST

A free-spirited musician came to see the Rebbe to discuss his idea of self-expression. During the conversation, the young man declared, somewhat brashly, "Rebbe, I can't stand following any kind of law or being told what to do; I have a powerful anarchic streak in me."

Bracing himself for a sermon, he was shocked when the Rebbe answered, his eyes smiling, "Don't we all?"

"This aspect of ourselves is called the *yetzer hara* or 'animal soul,'" explained the Rebbe, "and it's in order to harness this energy for the good that we descend into this world."

> *"The whole point of* Chasidism *is to transform the nature of one's character traits."*
> —RABBI SHNEUR ZALMAN OF LIADI[16]

SPECIAL DELIVERY

Visiting Detroit on business, a *chasid* from London met a Jewish man who asked him about the *mitzvah* of *tefillin*. The *chasid* patiently answered the man's questions and then asked him if he owned a pair. "I don't," replied the man, "but if I did, I'd put them on every day."

There and then, the *chasid* decided he'd give the man a pair of *tefillin*. "When I return to Detroit in six weeks, I'm going to bring them to you," he concluded. On his way back to London, the *chasid* stopped in New York and wrote a note to the Rebbe about the encounter.

The next morning, the Rebbe's secretary handed the *chasid* an urgent note. After blessing him with success, the Rebbe wrote, "Is it right that a Jew who put on *tefillin* yesterday—perhaps for the first time in years—should wait six weeks for you to bring him a pair?"

"Please buy the *tefillin* today, and if you can send them to Detroit in time for him to put them on today, do so. If not, please go back to Detroit yourself and help him put the *tefillin* on today—even if it means you won't be home on Shabbat."

The Rebbe concluded, "When this Jew sees how much it means to you that he has *tefillin* right away, this *mitzvah* will have a special importance to him."

Passion is caught, not taught.

THE RABBINATE, RE-DEFINED

Before embarking on a rabbinic career, a newly-ordained rabbi came to see the Rebbe for advice. "The role and objectives of a rabbi have changed from what they were in previous generations," the Rebbe remarked.

"In what way?" asked the young man.

"In the past, a rabbi would wait in the synagogue for congregants to come to him for guidance and instruction. Today a rabbi can no longer do that. Rabbis must go out and look for ways to reach and inspire people outside of the synagogue. If in the past a rabbi's job was to *respond* to people's interest in Judaism, today he must *create* that interest.

"Furthermore," the Rebbe continued, "the rabbinate used to be a job. Today it must be more than that. Even when a rabbi is successful at building a congregation, he should not become satisfied with his achievements, but should continue to reach out to those who are not yet connected to Jewish life."

Is it a career or a calling?

THE MASTER PLAN

The son of a *chasid* who was hospitalized just before
the High Holidays visited the Rebbe before Yom Kippur to
receive a piece of honey cake, per Jewish custom. Smiling,
the Rebbe handed him a piece of cake and said, "Give this
to your father and may G-d bless him with a sweet and
healthy year."

The Rebbe continued earnestly, "Tell your father that
when he finishes the mission for which he was sent to the
hospital, G-d will set him free from there."

Inspired by the Rebbe's message relayed by his son, the
man proceeded to initiate conversations with his doctors
and fellow patients regarding their spiritual well-being.

The day after Yom Kippur, the Rebbe sent his personal
secretary to visit the man in the hospital. His first question
was: "The Rebbe wants to know, have you completed your
mission here yet?"

---

*The way to answer
"What do I do?" is to ask,
"Why am I truly here?"*

CONNECTING TO THE DIVINE

FABRIC OF LIFE

During a Shabbat *chasidic* gathering led by the Rebbe, a man from Montreal—a dry cleaner by profession—was present. During his talk, the Rebbe dwelt on the spiritual lessons to be learned from dry cleaning.

"Before being worn, a garment is completely clean and smooth. After it is used for a while, it becomes creased and dirty. Of course, one does not throw away the item, but takes it to the cleaners regularly. To treat it, the dry cleaner places it in a machine with a hot liquid and soaks it in cleaning agents to remove the grime. Afterwards, he irons the garment, pressing it with a weight.

"When G-d gives a *neshamah* to a Jew, it is pure, as we say in our daily morning prayers: 'The soul You have given me is pure.' With time, though, it tends to become 'creased' and dirty from its exposure to materialism and selfishness."

"In order to remove the dirt that has accumulated, the soul requires a cleansing process. First, we immerse it in the heat of heartfelt prayer and Torah study—both of which are compared to water.

"Then, we place the 'weight' of the *mitzvot* upon ourselves, which initially may seem a heavy burden, but ultimately it 'irons out' the *neshamah* and returns it to its original unblemished condition."

"I offer thanks to You, living and eternal King, for You have mercifully restored my soul within me; Your faithfulness is great."

—PRAYER UPON AWAKENING FROM SLEEP

THE RIGHT QUESTION

A young musician on a spiritual quest once approached the Rebbe as he was getting out of his car in front of Lubavitch headquarters.

"I have a question," he exclaimed in the Yiddish of his youth.

"What is it?" the Rebbe asked.

"Where is G-d?" he asked.

"Everywhere," the Rebbe replied.

"I know," the young man continued, "But where?"

"In everything and in every place," said the Rebbe, "In a tree, in a stone…"

The young man persisted, "I know, but *where*?"

"In your heart—if that's how you're asking."

"Where is G-d?
Wherever you let Him in."
—THE KOTZKER REBBE[17]

A BIG MIRACLE

Having emigrated from the Soviet Union with great difficulty, a couple visited the Rebbe for a blessing. The woman broke down in tears. "Why are you crying?" the Rebbe asked, caringly.

"I just received a letter from my sister who remains trapped in Russia," she said. "Her husband, who had been incarcerated, was just notified by the KGB that their family would never be given permission to leave the country!"

"From the KGB's point of view," the Rebbe responded, "you too should still be in Russia. Why are you here? Because G-d performed a miracle and took you out of there. Although your sister might need a bigger miracle than your family did, do you think that for G-d a 'big miracle' is more difficult to perform than a 'small miracle?'"

Six months later, the woman's sister and her family were allowed to emigrate to the United States.

---

*Don't project your
limitations onto G-d.*

A GOOD REPUTATION

A philanthropist who had funded a Jewish day school had subsequently fallen on hard times. He wrote a long letter to the Rebbe bemoaning his circumstances.

"Due to recent business challenges, my reputation has become tarnished," he wrote, "and I am finding it extremely difficult to do business."

The Rebbe circled the words, "My reputation has become tarnished," and wrote in the margin: "In the eyes of G-d, the Master and Provider of the entire world, as a result of your having established an institution where His children are brought closer to Him, your reputation is absolutely stellar."

A good reputation is a vessel for blessing. A G-dly reputation is a source of blessing.

EFFECTIVE ADVERTISING

During the 1960s a newly-appointed campus rabbi
placed an advertisement in the university paper promoting
his activities and offerings on the upcoming holiday. The
clever ad called on Jewish students to "Take up arms for the
cause of liberty, like your radical ancestors in Egypt," and
played on contemporary themes which would resonate with
the students.

Proud of the modern design and clever terminology, the
rabbi sent a copy of the ad to the Rebbe, expecting to be
congratulated.

The Rebbe sent back the following message: "In future
advertisements for Jewish festivals, remember to mention
the relevant *mitzvot* that must be fulfilled."

---

*Don't get so carried away
with the inspiration that you
leave out the information.*

ANGER MANAGEMENT

A young pediatrician who treated chronically ill children once visited the Rebbe. He confessed that he was troubled, sometimes even angered, by questions of why G-d allows such suffering.

After a conversation on the meaning of suffering, the Rebbe said pointedly, "If you are angry at G-d, you may be harming the child's chances for a miracle. Instead of being angry with G-d, be grateful for the opportunity to be involved in a miracle.

"This," sighed the Rebbe, "might help bring about the miracle."

Faith is the human miracle we give G-d. Healing is the divine miracle He gives us back.

SACRED BUSINESS

A rabbi who was also a successful businessman once asked the Rebbe whether it would be advisable for him to leave business in order to focus exclusively on outreach.

To his surprise, the Rebbe encouraged him to remain in business, explaining, "Business, too, is a vehicle for sanctifying G-d's Name. Through your business activities you will influence Jews you would not have been able to reach as a rabbi."

"Know Him in all your ways."
—PROVERBS[18]

A SCIENTIST'S DIARY

An acclaimed professor and scientist was in a private audience with the Rebbe, and the discussion turned to the principle of 'Divine Providence.'

"Have you ever come across the teaching of the Baal Shem Tov that everything we see and hear is designed by Heaven to bring us closer to G-d?" the Rebbe asked.

"I have," replied the professor.

"Of all people, a scientist is best positioned to observe Divine Providence in action."

"Really?" asked the professor, surprised.

"Yes. You study the complexities of nature and you meet experts in all fields of scientific exploration. You must have a wealth of stories and impressions, many of them containing lessons for life and demonstrating the workings of Providence."

"I'd like to ask you for personal favor," concluded the Rebbe. "You should keep a journal and record these stories and events, as well as your reflections and the lessons that you learn from them in the service of G-d. And if you have trouble deciphering the meaning of any of these occurrences, please come see me, and I'll be happy to analyze them together with you."

"You will seek Me and find Me when you search for Me with all your heart."—JEREMIAH [19]

NOURISHING FAITH

A writer who was doing research on a book about Jewish mysticism and spirituality visited the Rebbe to discuss his project and gain insight. During their conversation about living with faith he blurted out, "Rebbe, I don't know anybody who wouldn't *like* to have faith—but how can one get faith if they don't have it?"

The Rebbe responded, "Faith is not something you have or don't have; it's something you must always work toward. And like the physical body, which needs to be fed daily in order to stay alive, the soul, too, needs to be nourished every day.

"How is the soul nourished and fed? Through study, prayer, and constantly reinforcing a sense of trust in the Creator."

Faith is not a gift,
it's a goal.

ONE FOR ALL AND ALL FOR ONE

Mr. Elliot Lasky, a spiritual seeker, once came to see the Rebbe with a burning question.

"In our prayers we proclaim, 'Hear O Israel, *Hashem* is our G-d, *Hashem* is One.'[20] Rebbe, '*Hashem* is One' seems like a universal statement! Why does the Torah single out the People of Israel?

"How can it be said that the Creator of all is 'our' G-d? Isn't there only one G-d for all peoples, whether you're a Jew, an African, or an Indian?"

The Rebbe replied: "The essence of an African is to be who he truly is as an African; the essence of an Indian is to be who he truly is as an Indian. And the essence of a Jew is to be bound to G-d through His Torah and *mitzvot*."

Every nation has a language; learn the language of your soul.

LOSING YOURSELF

A young man from France once visited the Rebbe
to discuss his spiritual well-being. "Rebbe," he said,
"Whenever I think about myself and reflect on my spiritual
state, I become unhappy with what I see. I feel like I can't
achieve happiness based on what I see in myself."

The Rebbe responded, "When you are unhappy, reflect
upon the fact that you are but a finite creature whom the
Creator has given the privilege to be bound with Him
through the *mitzvot*."

*Real joy comes from
stepping out of yourself,
and into the Infinite.*

A CONSTANT COMPANION

A man's young granddaughter was flying from London to New York, and he was anxious about it. He decided to request the Rebbe's blessing for the child, who was "traveling as an unaccompanied minor."

In response, the Rebbe simply crossed out the prefix 'un' in the word "unaccompanied" and added the phrase "...by *Hashem.*" The man's note was returned to him, now stating: "My granddaughter is traveling accompanied by *Hashem.*"

"...I fear no evil, for You are with me."
—PSALMS[21]

SEEING IS BELIEVING

A short time after the Six Day War, an individual was reporting to the Rebbe on his trip to Israel. The Rebbe commented: "I hope you weren't influenced by certain media where Israel is portrayed as a secular society. In my view, an Israeli who tells you he is an atheist doesn't really mean it in his heart of hearts.

"If a person observes open miracles, is it possible to remain an atheist?"

*"The Jews are believers,
the children of believers."*
—TALMUD[22]

JEWISH CONTINUITY

"What is the secret to Jewish survival?" a man asked the Rebbe. "How have the Jews survived longer than any other people, and under such impossible conditions?"

The Rebbe guided the man to the words of Jeremiah, who compares the survival of the Jews to the laws of nature:

"...If these laws (of nature) depart from before Me, says G-d, so will the seed of Israel cease being a nation before Me for all time."[23]

"This shows that the eternal existence of the Jewish People has been assured to us by G-d," explained the Rebbe. "However, the *identification* of Jews with this destiny can only be assured through their unwavering connection to the Torah."

The real question is not whether the Jewish People will survive, but what part you will play in their story.

IN G-D WE TRUST

A businessman from London who faced a financial crisis once visited the Rebbe for his counsel and blessing. "I had hoped to meet under different circumstances," he said to the Rebbe, handing him several papers outlining his business problems.

After reading through the report, the Rebbe gave the man some practical advice and then turned the conversation to spiritual matters.

"Do you know what *emunah* is?" the Rebbe asked.

"Yes," said the man, "faith in G-d."

"Do you know the difference between *emunah*—faith, and *bitachon*—trust?"

"No," replied the man.

"Allow me to explain," said the Rebbe. "Trust is not simply a higher form of faith. It's something quite different.

"When a person with faith is confronted with a problem, he believes G-d will help him overcome it. But a person with trust doesn't see his difficulties as *problems* in the first place, because he trusts that G-d doesn't send problems, only *challenges.*"

The real believer doesn't see obstacles, only opportunities.

A FOUNDATIONAL TRUTH

To mark the Jewish holiday of *Lag B'omer*, the Rebbe
would encourage *chasidim* to organize public parades
celebrating Jewish identity and tradition.

One year, the organizers of the parades in Israel
submitted some of the signs they had prepared to be
reviewed by the Rebbe. One of the banners advertised a
recent campaign which the Rebbe had initiated, calling
on Jewish children to participate in the writing of a Torah
scroll by "purchasing" a letter. The sign proclaimed, "I have
a letter in the Children's Torah Scroll," and showed three
children each holding a letter of the Hebrew alphabet.

Upon reviewing the sign, the Rebbe inquired, "Why
are the children holding the letters *Bet, Shin,* and *Lamed,*
specifically?"

The Rebbe was told, "The *Bet* and *Lamed* represent the
first and last letter of the Torah, and the *Shin* represents the
first letter in the central Jewish prayer, *Shema Yisrael.*"

"I would suggest that the letters *Aleph, Mem,* and *Tav* be featured instead. Together they spell out the word *emet,* meaning 'truth.' Truthfulness, honesty and integrity are the foundation of education.

"In fact, the word *emet* is made up of the very first, middle and last letters of the Hebrew alphabet—teaching us that truth is not consistent unless it is true through and through, from the beginning, through the middle, and until the end."

The commitment to truth is the first step on the path of spiritual development.

PRACTICE MAKES PERFECT

An academic once visited the Rebbe to discuss his questions in Kabbalah and Jewish mysticism.

The Rebbe offered: "Studying Kabbalah and Jewish mysticism as if it were a secular field, like mathematics or physics, is futile. The way to understand the depths of the *mitzvot* is to perform them. These actions, repeated many times, will form the basis for the knowledge that you are seeking.

"Imagine you never tasted sugar, and you read many books on how sweet sugar is. It's all theory until you actually put a sugar cube into your mouth, at which point no more explanation is needed."

The path to understanding is action.

LOVE AND RELATIONSHIPS

G-D'S WORK

The Rebbe was once addressing a women's convention. In middle of passionately encouraging the women to continue their activism on behalf of the Jewish people, he stopped and said earnestly:

"...But when a woman dresses her children in fresh clothing, feeds her children nutritious food, and goes around her home at night making sure that the windows are closed and no draft is blowing on her child, this, too, is *avodat Hashem*—the holy work of serving G-d!"

If building communities is holy work, building children is 'holy of holies.'

MARRIAGE ADVICE

In a personal conversation, the Rebbe got the sense that a visitor had difficulty making commitments. "Why aren't you married yet?" the Rebbe asked, kindly.

"I don't feel like I'm ready for marriage," replied the young man.

"Getting married is like learning to swim," the Rebbe said. "You don't learn to swim by reading a book about swimming; you have to jump in the water. The same is true for marriage; you learn about marriage by being married."

Some things in life can be learned only by doing.

GIVE AND TAKE

A man sought advice from the Rebbe on how to help a family member with an issue of self-restraint. The Rebbe guided him, saying, "Know, when you take something negative away from someone, you must be sure to replace it with something positive. If not, a void will be created, and another form of negativity may come to fill it."

Don't repress, redirect.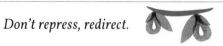

THE BEST MAN

A young man who was engaged to be married visited the Rebbe for a blessing. In passing he mentioned that, being a clarinetist, he planned to regale his wedding guests with a performance. The Rebbe responded, "I would suggest that you don't do the entertaining at your own wedding. Your wedding is like a personal Yom Kippur.

"I myself had wanted to spend time with each of the distinguished guests at my wedding. My father-in-law, the Previous Rebbe, discouraged this, telling me it was not the appropriate time."

Weddings are intended to elevate the bride and groom, not to entertain the guests.

INCLUSIVITY

A couple came to ask the Rebbe for a blessing for a child who had become engaged. After receiving a blessing, they began to leave when the Rebbe called them back: "And what of your other children? Are they not in need of a blessing?"

"Many people are waiting to see you," said the man, "and we didn't want to take up your time with non-urgent requests."

The Rebbe said, "When one child has a celebration, the others can sometimes feel left out. It's important, as you plan this wedding that you include your other children and make sure they don't feel neglected."

Don't let the joy of one of your children come at the expense of the others.

SELF-REFINEMENT

A newly married *chasid* suggested to the Rebbe that he might increase certain religious stringencies in his home. These practices would inevitably impose more restrictive behaviors on his wife as well.

While the Rebbe encouraged his yearning for spiritual service, he offered the young man some pointed guidance: "When you strive to go higher, start with practices that demand of yourself, not of others."

It's called self-refinement *for a reason.*

THE PERFECT MATCH

A boy had reached marriageable age, and his mother had set her heart on a certain young woman for him. She went to the Rebbe for his blessing on the match. "Although they are both wonderful people," said the Rebbe, "I don't think she's an ideal match for your son."

"But how can that be?" the mother exclaimed, "They are two really wonderful people. Doesn't it make sense that they should marry each other?"

"Is a glass of cold milk not refreshingly delicious?"

"Yes," she replied hesitantly.

"And does a nice cut of meat not taste good?"

"It does," she had to admit.

"And yet," the Rebbe continued, "though they may be wonderful on their own, the Torah tells us that these two foods should not be brought together."

Are you looking for what's 'best,' or what's right for you?

COMMON GROUND

An activist came to see the Rebbe to discuss a topic that was a matter of grave concern to the Rebbe, but it had also become a point of contention within the Jewish community. The visitor was critical of a certain Jewish leader because of his lenient stance on a fundamental issue in Jewish law, and suggested breaking off his working relationship with him.

The Rebbe disagreed. "It's true that on this one *mitzvah* we differ, but there are another 612 *mitzvot* on which we can work together!"

No matter your differences,
you can always find common ground.

HEART TO HEART

A man who was well-versed in Jewish mysticism came to the Rebbe. In the course of the conversation, the Rebbe brought up the *mitzvah* to 'love your fellow as yourself.'

"What are you doing to help the Jewish community?" asked the Rebbe.

"I'm thinking about doing more."

The Rebbe responded, "Kabbalah and Jewish law views the right side as more dominant. For example, the right hand should be used to perform a *mitzvah*. This is because the right side represents *chesed*, 'loving-kindness,' whereas the left side represents *gevurah*, 'withholding.'

"Why then did G-d place our heart, 'the source of loving-kindness' on the left side of our body?

"You see," continued the Rebbe, "your heart is actually on the 'right side!' The job of your heart is to empathize with, and care for, others. So when you stand facing another person, from their perspective, your heart is on the right side."

Spiritual giants are set apart, by the way in which they use their heart.

A VESSEL FOR BLESSING

A couple that was childless for over ten years were at a loss of what to do. A friend suggested they write a letter to the Rebbe and ask for a blessing.

The Rebbe replied: "If at the time of your marriage, either of you might have hurt someone's feelings through a broken engagement or promise, it might be necessary to obtain their forgiveness."

After extensive research, the couple determined that a woman peripherally involved with arranging their match had expected compensation from the two parties. The couple had been unaware of this, and the woman went unrewarded. After receiving her forgiveness for the misunderstanding, the couple was blessed with four children.

"There is no better vessel for blessing than peace."
—MISHNAH[24]

LOVE IS THE ANSWER

A man who had survived the Holocaust poured out his heart to the Rebbe: "My entire family was murdered. I cannot sleep at night, because I'm reliving the horrors I've seen. I have decided never to get married and bring children into this dark world."

The Rebbe looked deeply into his eyes, and said, "Given your terrible loss, I understand your feelings. Just know that your entire family is watching you, and they care deeply about you.

"If you live the life of a dead person, you are continuing the tragedy of their death. If you live a life of love, you will bring them some comfort."

"But I cannot get married!" the man insisted. "I just don't trust people any more."

"You can always love children," the Rebbe said. "Find a way to show them unconditional love, and this will bring light back into your life. Even on the hard days, when you're not in the mood, just do it."

The man took the Rebbe's advice to heart, and could be seen distributing candies and good cheer to the children in his synagogue until the day of his passing.

Loving is living.

SHARING GOOD NEWS

The Rebbe once followed up with an individual who had asked for a blessing for someone undergoing a difficult challenge. "How is he doing?" the Rebbe asked.

"Thank G-d, everything worked out in the end," the man answered.

"Why is it," said the Rebbe, "that people freely share their bad news, but fail to follow up when there is good news?"

Those who love you want to hear from you.
Not only when you're in need, but also when you succeed.

A PARENT'S ROLE

The Rebbe spoke to a man who had recently celebrated the weddings of his children: "Allow me to share some advice. Do not mix into the affairs of your grown children. If they consult you, you may advise them, but never impose yourself on them. It's their life, and it's their decision how to live it."

Our children are not our own,
but are given to us on loan.
Our role is to facilitate, not force,
inspire, not impose,
coach, not control.

A SPECIAL LOVE

The Rebbe shared a story with a group of *yeshivah* students. Once, a rabbi had questioned his father-in-law's nonjudgmental approach toward Jews who were far from faith.

"My father-in-law replied: 'All parents were created with the capacity to love each of their children, no matter how many. And yet, if one of them were lacking in some way, they would not love this child any less than the others, G-d forbid. To the contrary, they would extend a special love for this child precisely because of their deficit. The same is true with regards to our brethren who didn't have the benefit of a Jewish education; we must embrace them with even more love, not less.'"

Don't judge, love.

JEWISH
LEADERSHIP

THE ONLY WAY

A rabbi was visiting with the Rebbe just after the Six Day War, and the conversation turned to the situation in Israel. "In my view," said the Rebbe, "the overtly miraculous nature of this war indicates that these are extraordinary times. If only these events inspire more Jews to return to their roots, it can bring about *Mashiach's* arrival."

"But there is another way for *Mashiach* to come," the rabbi said. "The Talmud states that *Mashiach* will come as a result of a generation being either completely righteous, or completely unrighteous."

The Rebbe retorted passionately: "There's no way that I will allow the latter to happen!"

A true leader believes in his followers, more than they believe in themselves.

A SPIRITUAL APPETITE

A rabbi, an elite scholar from Europe, had opened a synagogue in Brooklyn. He visited the Rebbe for guidance.

"No matter what I do, I have trouble gathering a regular *minyan* for Shabbat services," he complained. "What do you recommend?"

"Do you serve hot *cholent* after services?"

"No," he replied.

"Then I would suggest that you do so," said the Rebbe with a smile.

From that meeting onward, every week the Rebbe would send the rabbi a check with a generous sum for the hot *cholent*. The *minyan* flourished for many years.

Don't forget to be practical.

SEIZE THE MOMENT

After learning that there was no Jewish high school in Mexico, a young rabbinical student was inspired to open a *yeshivah* there himself. He visited several Jewish leaders to receive their guidance and blessing, but was met with skepticism.

Disheartened, he found himself in a private audience with the Rebbe one Thursday night, and poured out his heart.

"In my view," said the Rebbe passionately, "not only should you go ahead with this mission, but you should do so immediately. If possible, you should leave for Mexico tomorrow morning so you can plant the seeds of a Jewish high school there even before Shabbat!"

---

*Anything worth doing
is worth doing now.*

THE IMPORTANCE OF DIVERSITY

In the 1950s, a Jewish children's magazine provided stimulating educational reading and Torah values to many. Chabad had its own publication, called *Talks and Tales*, with similar objectives.

The non-Lubavitch publication was struggling financially. When the Rebbe learned that they were considering discontinuing their publication, he sent a check for the amount needed to keep the magazine running.

"But aren't they competitors?" the Rebbe was asked.

"The Jewish community is diverse," the Rebbe responded. "People's needs, persuasions and interests vary. It's crucial that there is something for everyone."

If it's about you, the others are competition.
If it's about serving the Divine cause, they're all parts of one grand composition.

THE PITFALL OF PERFECTIONISM

A community leader once visited the Rebbe to discuss an issue he had with Lubavitch. "Rebbe, while I admire the efforts of Lubavitch to rejuvenate Jewish life around the world, I take issue with the fact that they allow the newly-observant to become teachers themselves so soon. These people are still in the process of learning, and they might inadvertently teach things incorrectly or even misrepresent Judaism to others."

The Rebbe sighed. "You make a valid point. And indeed, in ideal times yours would be the correct approach. But when there's a fire, anybody who can carry a bucket of water is enlisted to put it out.

"There's a fire raging," the Rebbe continued with emotion, "and so many of our brothers and sisters are at risk of being lost to assimilation. Today, anyone with access to water must do whatever they can to put out the fire."

Don't allow the desire to do something perfectly get in the way of doing it at all.

CREDIT

Professor Velvl Greene, a celebrated biologist, met with the Rebbe before delivering a lecture to a group of Jewish scientists. The Rebbe asked him to share a certain insight in his talk but to refrain from quoting him as its source.

The Rebbe explained: "In Torah scholarship, it is important to quote your sources. Indeed, doing so hastens the Redemption.[25] However, in this case, it might get in the way; it's much more important that this insight be effective than that I be credited for it."

Do you want your idea to spread far? Let it go.

A PUBLIC SERVANT

Mr. Robert Abrams, an attorney general of New York, once presented the Rebbe with a written proclamation, honoring him for his "extraordinary work around the world."

The Rebbe responded, "It's not me—it's the movement!"

A true leader doesn't see his constituents as his platform, he sees himself as theirs.

HOMELAND SECURITY

At a time when there was an outburst of vandalism
in synagogues and religious institutions in Southern
California, a *shliach* in the area wrote to the Rebbe asking if
the Rebbe's previous directive to keep the doors open 24/7
still applied.

The Rebbe circled the words "religious institutions in
Southern California" and wrote, "From now on, you should
follow the protocol of the religious institutions in your
area."

*Believe in miracles
but don't rely on them.*

POWER OF INTENTION

The Rebbe once suggested that a certain young man become a rabbi and community activist. "But Rebbe," he countered, "I'm not sure I have what it takes to be successful as a community leader."

"Know this," the Rebbe responded, "if your intentions are pure, you have what you need to be a leader. If you will do what you do not for your own sake but for the sake of the community, this merit itself will make you successful."

Sincerity is more important than sophistication.

THE KEY TO SUCCESS

A supporter of Chabad activities once presented the Rebbe with the key to his local Chabad House. "Rebbe," he said passionately, "we want you to have this key so that you can feel comfortable visiting our Chabad House day or night!"

The Rebbe responded warmly, "I would feel most comfortable if you would take the key back and open your doors wide so that every Jew feels comfortable visiting your Chabad House twenty-four hours a day, seven days a week!"

There are no 'hours' or 'off-limits' when it comes to family. Every Jew is your family.

TRUSTING YOUR ABILITIES

A newly ordained rabbi asked the Rebbe a difficult question in Jewish law. His wife had recently given birth to twin boys and the *mohel* didn't know whether to recite a separate blessing over each of the circumcisions, or one blessing for both, so he asked the Rebbe what to do.

"You studied to be a rabbi," the Rebbe said, encouragingly, "why don't you research the issue and come to your own *Halachic* conclusion?"

After researching the relevant sources, the rabbi shared his ruling with the Rebbe.

The Rebbe said with a bright smile, "That's the same conclusion I had come to myself."

Sometimes, you need to take a step back to help another step forward.

FAMILY FIRST

In the late 1960s, a Jewish chaplain on a college campus turned to the Rebbe for advice. "Many of the students are involved in protesting the Vietnam War. To what extent should I invest myself in anti-war and human rights demonstrations, when they come at the expense of my Jewish programming?

The Rebbe responded: "You have a responsibility to bring benefit to every human being. At the same time, you must consider the priorities presented you by your current circumstances.

"If two people were drowning, and one was a stranger and you could save only one of them, wouldn't your brother come first?"

"The poor of your own city come first."—TALMUD[26]

THE THEORY OF RELATIVITY

The organizers of a Chabad school production once asked the Rebbe if a certain genre of music could be considered appropriate for their show.

"Why not go with a higher spiritual standard when it's possible to do so?" said the Rebbe.

One of the organizers asked, "But didn't you approve that same genre when a different school asked your advice?"

"The advice I give differs from case to case, and from community to community," responded the Rebbe. "I offer guidance only when I feel that people will listen. When I sense that it won't be heeded, I refrain from giving directives."

> *"Just as it is a* mitzvah
> *to say that which will be*
> *accepted, it is a* mitzvah *to*
> *refrain from saying things*
> *that will not be accepted."*
> —TALMUD[27]

NO MONOPOLY

In response to a letter written by Dr. Robert Wilkes, in which he congratulated the Rebbe and his emissaries for their exceptional dedication and "concern for every Jewish individual," the Rebbe wrote:

"Needless to say, such appreciation is very gratifying, but I must confess and emphasize that this is not an original Lubavitch idea, for it is basic to Torah Judaism."

If you truly love your fellow as yourself, you would want them to be loved by everyone, not just loved by you.

SUBCONSCIOUS AGENDA

The Rebbe once asked a *chasid* who was traveling to Israel for personal reasons to visit certain Lubavitch institutions and report back. Upon his return, the Rebbe asked the *chasid* how much the travel expenses were.

The *chasid*, a man of means, replied, "I was hoping to have the merit of covering the costs myself."

"I'm sorry, but I can't agree to that," the Rebbe said.

Seeing the bewilderment on the *chasid*'s face, the Rebbe explained: "The Talmud[28] disqualifies the High Priest from serving on the tribunal that decides on whether to declare a leap year.

"You see, the sages were concerned that he might subconsciously refrain from declaring an extra month to the calendar for personal reasons. On Yom Kippur the High Priest needed to immerse in the *mikveh* several times, and the later Yom Kippur is, the colder the water would be. Look to what extremes the Torah goes to in order to rule out even a remote possibility of a conflict of interest!

"If you expend personal funds for a communal initiative today, there may come a day when you will be involved in a different project for which you have to lay out funds, and you might choose not to, based on the subconscious concern that you won't be reimbursed."

No one is above a conflict of interest.

COMMANDER ON THE BRIDGE

A leading rabbi stationed in Pretoria, South Africa spoke to the Rebbe about his life-long dream of making *aliyah* to Israel. The Rebbe advised him to stay in his community, explaining, "As their leader and role model, your community needs you."

Sensing the rabbi's dismay, the Rebbe asked. "Are you planning to take my advice?"

"I have a military background," said the rabbi, "and in the Army there's a principle: when a soldier comes to a general and receives an order, he must listen. I've come to a general, I've gotten my orders, and I now know what I have to do."

The Rebbe replied: "My experience is with the Navy, working on ships. The captain of a ship cannot be the first one off the ship; he has to care for everyone under his command. This is your job, and why you must stay."

The Rebbe grew serious and said: "But I do not want you to stay because you 'received an order.' You should do it out of conviction and with love."

Three years later, the rabbi returned. As he walked in, the Rebbe greeted him and asked, "Are you still in Pretoria?"

"Yes."

"Out of conviction?"

"Yes."

The Rebbe's eyes twinkled. "And with love?"

A true leader doesn't impose but inspires.

STAY FOCUSED

A professor who was beginning to explore his Jewish roots wrote a letter to the Rebbe challenging the Torah's position on evolution. Over the next couple of months, whenever he wrote to the Rebbe about personal matters he received a prompt response, but the Rebbe never replied to his polemics on evolution, leading him to assume that the Rebbe had conceded to his arguments.

A few years passed, during which the professor made great strides in his Jewish observance. One day, he received a letter from the Rebbe and in the postscript, the Rebbe began to answer the professor's challenges one by one.

The Rebbe explained the reason he didn't reply to the professor's challenges earlier: "Previously, I wrote to you in reserved and guarded terms. Inasmuch as my purpose is to inspire greater adherence to Judaism, I try to avoid anything which might deter some individuals from a deeper commitment to *Yiddishkeit*. Now, I sense that you are ready for the answers."

Don't be right,
be wise.

ESSENCE OF THE LAW

The Rebbe asked a visiting businessman how his livelihood was faring. The man was reluctant to take the Rebbe's time for mundane matters. Sensing his hesitation, the Rebbe shared a story that happened during the intermediate days of Sukkot, during which Jewish law discourages worldly actions such as writing in order to protect the joy and sanctity of the festival.

"One *Chol Hamoed* day I entered the office of my father-in-law, the Previous Rebbe, and was surprised to see him writing a letter. Glimpsing the letter more closely, I was even more surprised to see that it was about the recipient's employment.

"I asked him how he allowed himself to write a letter on *Chol Hamoed* on so mundane a matter. My father-in-law replied: '*Zayn gashmiyus iz mayn ruchniyus*'—his material concern is my spiritual concern."

> *"A soul may descend to this world for seventy or eighty years just to do one favor for another person."*
> —THE BAAL SHEM TOV[29]

· ACKNOWLEDGEMENTS ·

It has been noted that there are two different types of philosophers: "i.e. philosophers" and "e.g. philosophers." "i.e." is an abbreviation of the latin word which means "in other words" and "e.g." is an abbreviation for the latin words which mean "for the sake of example."

"i.e." thinkers focus on general principles and definitions, in contrast to "e.g." thinkers who focus on striking, real-life examples.

Put differently, you can learn about someone's worldview from their teachings, speeches, and writings; or you can learn about the way they understand the world and the human condition through their encounters with real people, dealing with relevant issues, in an often changing and challenging world.

And that is how this book differs from others, and is intended to read.

But for that to happen, it became clear to me that the stories could not be grounded upon hearsay, or merely be "based upon a true story."

This, in turn, led me to the archives of the *My Encounter with the Rebbe* project which, to date, contain the firsthand testimonies of over 1300 people describing their personal encounters with the Rebbe.

These interviews are the first-person source for this book, and their contribution to the historical accuracy of data relating to the Rebbe cannot be overstated.

In many ways, these accounts enabled me to go back in time and personally take part in those very encounters with the Rebbe.

I am deeply grateful to Rabbi Elkanah Shmotkin, the visionary behind Jewish Educational Media (JEM) and its driving force. In addition to founding the *My Encounter with the Rebbe* project and serving as its inspirational guide, Rabbi Shmotkin's stubborn attention to detail—in matters of content, as well as aesthetics—has helped make this book what it is. His vast experience and expertise in interpreting and presenting the Rebbe and his teachings were invaluable.

Rabbi Yechiel Cagen, director of the *My Encounter with the Rebbe* project, was responsible for recording much of the testimony cited here, along with his incredible team. They graciously assisted me with access to the archives.

It goes without saying that working with firsthand accounts comes with its own set of challenges. There is a delicate balancing act between content and form, authenticity and accessibility—between staying true to the sometimes fragmented accounts of an interviewee, while presenting a smooth and structured read. At times, I felt compelled to take the liberty of completing unfinished thoughts and half sentences, and in so doing, I faced the daunting risks that flow from subjective interpretation.

Even letters and talks of the Rebbe have been modified slightly to match the form of this book. Though I tried my best to render each story and quote faithfully, if I came up short, the fault lies with me. Equally, any errors of transmission are my own.

The stories have been reviewed by Rabbis Mendel Feller and Mendel Alperowitz, whose keen and discerning reading ensured that the stories remained true to their sources and to the historical record. I'd like to thank Mrs. Sheina Herz for her skilled proofreading. Thank you to Chanie Kaminker of Hannabi Creative, and Anita Soble for the beautiful layout and cover design. Thank you to Chanie Raskin for her eloquent touch and valuable input.

A special thanks to my editor Mattisyahu Brown whose purity, precision and expert editing has greatly enhanced this book.

On a personal note, I would like to dedicate this book to my wife and life partner, Chanale, whose unwavering support and clear thinking has helped bring this project into being. To borrow Rabbi Akiva's words to his students about his wife, Rachel: "What is mine and what is yours, is truly hers."

I would like to express my gratitude to G-d for our beautiful children, Musya, Dov, Ester and Zelig, who bring unlimited joy to our lives.

Additionally, I'd like to express an overwhelming debt of gratitude to my dear parents, Rabbi Yosef Yitzchak and Hindy Kalmenson, my beloved grandparents, Rabbi Sholom Ber and Sara Shanowitz, and to my dear father and mother-in-law, Rabbi Yosef and Tamara Katzman, for their constant counsel, love, and support. My life and that of my family is greatly enriched by their living example of Jewish and *chasidic* values.

My dear brothers and sisters, Chanie, Nechama Dina, Menucha, Yekusiel, and Moishy, I feel so blessed to have you in my life.

Finally, I'd like to express a profound debt of gratitude to the individual at the heart of these stories, the Rebbe, of righteous memory, himself. His example and teachings have helped shape my worldview and life's work, and continue to guide me daily, never ceasing to demand that I be the best and truest version of myself I can be.

—MENDEL KALMENSON

· ABOUT THE AUTHOR ·

Rabbi Mendel Kalmenson has authored numerous articles and essays on Jewish thought for Chabad.org. He recently published his second book, entitled "A Time To Heal: The Lubavitcher Rebbe's Response to Loss and Tragedy." He lives in London with his family, where he is the rabbi and executive director of Chabad Belgravia.

• ENDNOTES •

1. *Keter Shem Tov, 160.*
2. *Breishit Raba, 21:6.*
3. *Ethics of the Fathers, 1:15.*
4. *Exodus, 10:9.*
5. *Torah Ohr, Genesis 1b.*
6. *Ethics of the Fathers, 1:14.*
7. *Reb Mendel, 220.*
8. *Isaiah, 60:21.*
9. *R. Moshe Ibn Ezra, Shirat Yisrael, 156.*
10. *Ethics of the Fathers, 1:14.*
11. *Ethics of the Fathers, 1:17.*
12. *Ethics of the Fathers, 4:1.*
13. *Ethics of the Fathers, 5:21.*
14. *Rashi, Deuteronomy, 6:6.*
15. *Ethics of the Fathers, 1:3.*
16. *Likkutei Dibburim, 128.*
17. *Emet v'Emunah, p. 97.*
18. *Proverbs, 3:6.*
19. *Jeremiah, 29:13.*
20. *Deuteronomy, 6:4.*
21. *Psalms 23:4.*
22. *Talmud Shabbat, 97a.*
23. *Jeremiah, 31:35.*
24. *Mishnah Uktzin, 3:12.*
25. *Ethics of the Fathers, 6:6.*
26. *Talmud, Bava Metzia, 71a.*
27. *Talmud Yevamot, 65b.*
28. *Talmud Sanhedrin, 18b.*
29. *Keter Shem Tov, Hosafot, 209.*

· SOURCES ·

Mrs. Diane Abrams, *January 21, 2002*.

Dr. Ruth Benjamin, *September 30, 2014*.

Rabbi Nachman Bernhard, *January 17, 2011*.

Professor Herman Branover, *February 22, 2006*.

Dr. Stuart Ditchek, *July 25, 2013*.

Mr. Naftali Deutsch, *September 11, 2011*.

Rabbi Dovid Edelman, *July 22, 2008*.

Mr. Motti Eden, *March 10, 2010*.

Rabbi Mordechai Einbinder, *September 9, 2011*.

Rabbi Naftali Estulin, *September 8, 2011*.

Rabbi Pinchus Feldman, *March 20, 2015*.

Dr. Robert Feldman, *January 4, 2012*.

Rabbi Moshe Feller, *November 8, 2010*.

Mr. Louis Gavin, *August 24, 2014*.

Dr. Max Glassman, *May 12, 2015*.

Mr. Marvin Goldsmith, *September 9, 2011*.

Rabbi Yosef Goldstein, *August 14, 2001*.

Rabbi Joshua Gordon, *September 13, 2011*.

Rabbi Yisroel Gordon, *May 15, 2005*.

Professor Velvl Greene, *April 1, 2008*.

Mr. Mendel Greenbaum, *March 31, 2011*.

Rabbi Shmuel Greisman, *February 18, 2015*.

Mrs. Mariashi Groner, *February 17, 2015*.

Rabbi Rafael Grossman, *January 30, 2012*.

Rabbi Yitzchak Maier Gurary, *January 18, 2011*.

Rabbi Noson Gurary, *November 20, 2013*.

Rabbi Mordechai Gutnick, *May 5, 2013*.

Mr. Freddy Hager, *August 9, 2007*.

Professor Susan Handelman, *March 20, 2007*.

Rabbi Simon Jacobson, *May 27, 2015*.

Mrs. Tzivia Jacobson, *September 18, 2014*.

· SOURCES ·

Rabbi Avrohom Jaffe, *March 23, 2015.*
Rabbi David Lapin, *June 5, 2015.*
Mr. Elliot Lasky, *May 12, 2013.*
Rabbi Shmuel Lew, *August 15, 2007.*
Mrs. Masha Lipskar, *July 8, 2014.*
Rabbi Chaim Nisenbaum, *June 19, 2015.*
Rabbi Yehuda Leib Posner, *November 28, 2006.*
Rabbi Zushe Posner, *December 18, 2009.*
Mr. Bentzion Rader, *August 6, 2007.*
Mr. Charles Roth, *March 2, 2010.*
Mrs. Adeena Singer, *August 26, 2014.*
Rabbi Hershel Slansky, *July 10, 2014.*
Rabbi Moshe Stern, *June 14, 2012.*
Rabbi Nachman Sudak, *May 29, 2013.*
Mr. Michael Tabor, *March 23, 2015.*
Rabbi Joseph Telushkin, *February 16, 2011.*
Rabbi Tzvi Telsner, *June 20, 2014.*
Mrs. Shana Tiechtel, *February 4, 2015.*
Rabbi Marvin Tokayer, *December 8, 2010.*
Rabbi Moshe Tzur, *November 17, 2015.*
Mr. Lukas Van Der Walde, *June 26, 2014.*
Rabbi Tzvi Hersh Weinreb, *May 5, 2013.*
Rabbi Meshulam Weiss, *September 13, 2011.*
Rabbi Herbert Weiner, *May 1, 2007.*
Professor Robert Wilkes, *October 21, 2015.*
Rabbi Yosef Wineberg, *June 24, 2008.*
Rabbi Dr. Laibl Wolf, *November 16, 2008.*
Rabbi Pinchos Woolstone, *December 24, 2013.*
Rabbi Boruch Zaichyk, *May 5, 2013.*
Rabbi Mordechai Zajac, *February 9, 2010.*
Rabbi Shlomo Zarchi, *April 23, 2013.*

· GLOSSARY ·

770: Shorthand for 770 Eastern Parkway, the address of Chabad's world headquarters in Brooklyn, New York.

Ahavat Yisrael: Love your fellow Jew.

Aliyah: Immigration to the Land of Israel.

Baal Shem Tov: The name given to Rabbi Yisrael ben Eliezer (1698-1760), founder of Chasidism.

Bimah: A raised table at which the Torah is publicly read in the synagogue, and from which a sermon is delivered.

Chasid/chasidic/chasidism: Derived from the Hebrew word for 'pious,' a follower of *Chasidism*, the Movement founded by Rabbi Israel Baal Shem Tov (1698-1760). *Chasidism* refers to the movement's philosophy. A *chasid* approaches the commandments of Judaism with intense joy.

Chabad: The *chasidic* movement also known as 'Lubavitch.' An acronym for *chochmah, binah, daat,* "wisdom, understanding and knowledge," in Hebrew, representing the philosophy of the movement founded by Rabbi Schneur Zalman of Liadi.

Chol Hamoed: The intermediate days of Passover and Sukkot; "minor" days of the festival.

Cholent: A casserole-like dish prepared before the start of Shabbat. To avoid the prohibitions against cooking on Shabbat, it is kept warm from Friday afternoon, usually until Shabbat lunch.

Farbrengen/farbrenging: An informal *chasidic* gathering where friends encourage and assist one-another to improve their relationships with G-d and their contemporaries. In the case of the Rebbe's *farbrengen*, the event has the face of a public address and Torah discourse, bookended by chasidic melodies and toasts of *L'chaim!*

· GLOSSARY ·

Gelt: Money.

Kipah: The head covering worn by Jewish men symbolizing recognition of G-d above.

L'chaim: A toast or blessing, often exchanged over wine or other strong drink.

Halachah/halachic: Torah law.

Hashem: G-d.

Lag B'omer: The 33rd day of the counting of the Omer. Also commemorating the end of a plague which killed thousands of Rabbi Akiva's students. *Yahrzeit* of Rabbi Shimon bar Yochai, author of the Zohar, and day of celebrating his life.

Lubavitch: A small town in the county of Mohilev, White Russia, which served as the center of the Chabad Movement for four generations, from 1813-1915 and whose name has become synonymous with the movement.

Mikveh: A bathing pool in which a person immerses himself as part of the transition to ritual purity.

Minyan: A quorum of ten necessary for communal prayer.

Mitzvah/ mitzvot: The Hebrew word for "commandment," refers to the 613 commandments presented by G-d in the Torah. '*Mitzvot*' in the plural.

Mohel: The trained expert who performs ritual circumcisions.

Mashiach: Messiah. One of the 13 principles of the Jewish faith is that G-d will send the Messiah to return the Jews to the land of Israel, rebuild the Holy Temple and usher in the Era of *Mashiach*.

· GLOSSARY ·

Nachas: The quintessential Yiddish term referring to joy or pleasure, usually from one's children or grandchildren.

Seder: The order of service observed at home on the first night (first two nights in the Diaspora) of Passover.

Neshamah: Soul.

Shiva: The seven day mourning period following the funeral of a deceased next of kin.

Shliach mitzvah gelt: Money given to an individual to be given to a third person for charity.

Shliach/ shlucha/ shlichus: Emissary. In our case, referring to the young pairs of '*shliach*' and '*shlucha*,' male and female emissaries, whom the Rebbe would send to bring Torah and *mitzvot* to Jewish communities around the globe. *Shlucha* in feminine. *Shlichus* is the noun of going on the mission.

Simchat Torah: Festival immediately following Sukkot, on which the cycle of publicly reading the Torah is annually concluded and recommenced. It is observed with great joy, singing and the Hakafot procession with the Torah scrolls.

Sukkot: Festival of Tabernacles.

Talmud: The key text of rabbinical Judaism, which contains the basis of Jewish law.

Tzizit: Ritual fringed four-cornered garment.

Yeshivah: Torah academy.

Yiddishkeit: Torah-Judaism.

Zechut: Merit.

· MY ENCOUNTER WITH THE REBBE ·

Jewish Educational Media's *My Encounter with the Rebbe*
oral history project aims to document the life of the Rebbe,
Rabbi Menachem M. Schneerson, of righteous memory,
through first-person, videotaped, testimony.

The initiative attempts to study the Rebbe's life,
documenting the wisdom, sensitivity, and charisma
he displayed in his direct interactions with hundreds
of thousands of individuals, impacting their lives and,
ultimately, influencing the course of Judaism in his times.

To date, over 1,300 interviews have been conducted.
These recordings, along with the 25,000 pages of
transcripts, serve as an unparalleled primary resource for
the historic record, and as a source of inspiration for those
who wish to learn from and emulate the Rebbe's example.